1992 AND ALL THIS

1992 AND ALL THIS

by

MATTHEW STURGIS

with illustrations by the author

MACMILLAN
LONDON

Illo almo fratre A.J.S.

First published 1991 by
MACMILLAN LONDON LIMITED
Cavaye Place London SW10 9PG
and Basingstoke

Associated companies in Auckland, Delhi, Dublin, Gaborone,
Hamburg, Harare, Hong Kong, Johannesburg, Kuala Lumpur,
Lagos, Manzini, Melbourne, Mexico City, Nairobi, New York,
Singapore and Tokyo

ISBN 0-333-55106-0

A CIP catalogue record for this book is available from
the British Library

Typeset by Macmillan Production Limited
Printed in Hong Kong

Errata

Page 59
For Spinach *read* Spanish

Pages 50 and 88
For Beagle *read* Eagle

CONTENTS

ACKNOWLEDGEMENTS

M ANY people have helped in the preparation of this slim volume – too many to name in full. But I must give special thanks to Professor K. von Rieppel for her determined account of the Germany economy; to Dr David Blanche for his exposition of the Balkan Question; to Dom Ziegler for buying me lunch; to Miss Sibley for her patient refusal to compile an index; and, of course, to my editor Roland Philipps, who has overlooked the manuscript at every stage of its development. It goes without saying that any errors of fact or taste that have found their way into the finished work are entirely their responsibility.

And finally, I must acknowledge my largest debt – to my bank manager, Mr Stonyheart of Lloyds Bank (North London branch); it will, if sales go well, be paid off in monthly instalments.

FOREWARNED

THIS slim volume contains all the known facts (and both the known figures) about the countries of Europe – their geography, politics, culture and customs. Unknown facts have been vigorously expunged from the text so what remains should be well known to you already.

Although, on receiving the commission to write this work, I wasted no time in reading numerous reference books, I must acknowledge my debt to one important source. W. C. Sellar and R. J. Yeatman's pioneering volume *And Now All This* (sequel to *1066 And All That*) touches briefly but forcefully on the subject of European countries and I have borrowed freely from their instructive pages.

Originally this book was intended to cover only the member-countries of the EC, but cursory enquiries proved that no one could remember which countries were definitely in the Common Market and which were probably not. So the scope of the book was enlarged to offer a full and exhausting account of the Hole of Europe, in as far as it is memorable – or, at least, memorably European.

It is, nevertheless, to be hoped that this small but invaluable handbook (price £9.99) will provide the general reader with an up-to-date geo-political overview (as well, of course, as an hysterical perspective) in preparation for 1992, when Britain will finally 'Enter Europe' and become 'In Continent'.

FRANCE

FEW countries are so thoroughly European as France. Croques Monsieurs, Femmes Fatales, Enfants Terribles and even Bêtes Noires: all these decidedly foreign creatures exist in profusion just across the Channel (Fr. *Chanel*).

On the other hand, few countries possess so very little in the way of memorable geography. The coast is, of course, azure, but most of the interior is taken up with a massif central area of undefined colour and character.

To impose some geographical (and/or political) order on to this featureless mass the French have divided the country up into a series of Compartments named after memorable local wines (e.g. Champagne (Eng. countryside), Burgundy, Beaujolais, Claret, Piat d'Or, etc.).

These Departments (run by a succession of Maries, Chefs and Sommeliers) give ample scope for the French enthusiasm for bureaucracy (Eng. officiousness).

The President of France (Fr. *Président de Gaul*), in the meantime (and mainly in Paris), concentrates his political energies on not becoming confused with the Prime Minister of France or indeed the Mayor of Paris (pron. *Maree de Paree*). He is not always successful.

Economy

France, having so much countryside (Fr. *Champagne*), is decidedly agricultural. Much of France is given over to highly inflammable farmers. Like all farmers (and most Frenchmen) they complain incessantly (see The Great Whines of France) about:

(*a*) The excessive amount of weather (Fr. *l'heure* - not to be confused with *le temps* (Eng. time)).
(*b*) Imports of cheap British lamb.
(*c*) The woeful absence of weather (NB Fr. *temps*).
(*d*) The state of the 'Digestif system' (a complex system for ordering digestives at their local café).

Livestock: la vache qui rit, le mouton rothschild, le cochon bleu, le coq sportif, and even the rare mallard imaginaire.

Deadstock: l'agneau anglais brûlé.

Crops: grapes, gripes, petit pois (or *chic* peas).

For a vivid account of French agricultural life read *Le Grand Moan* or Proust's *A la Recherche du Temps Perdu* (Eng. *In Search of Lost Weather*).

Imports: Le Weekend, Le Smoking, Les amusing livres de Kilometres Kingville.

Exports: French kissing, French leave, French letters, French dressing (Fr. *Haute Couture*), *élan, éclat, je ne sais quoi*.

THE WHINES OF FRANCE: LE TEMPS

THE MOUTON ROTHSCHILD

Industry

France has a fine tradition of producing cheap but reliable motorcars: the slow Deux Chevaux; the even slower Deux Magots (which never moves at all and was, as a result, much used by the famous existentialist couple, the Marquis de Sartre and Simone de Boudoir); the very compact Citroën Pressé; and the rather larger Van Ordinaire.

Rail Travel

The French rail system is very impressive, with special commuter services (Fr. *Chemin d'Affaires*) and high-speed intercity trains (for departures see the *TGV Times*).

Paris boasts several magnificent railway stations: the Gare St Lazare, the Pont de Gare, the Coeur de Lyon and, in the middle of town, the Massif Central.

National Characteristics

The French have a tendency to be very French and to become obsessed with their obsessions (Fr. *Bidet Fixe*). Traditional French obsessions include: their lunch, their digestives, their digestions, their bidets. In spite of all this they do possess a certain Garlic Charm.

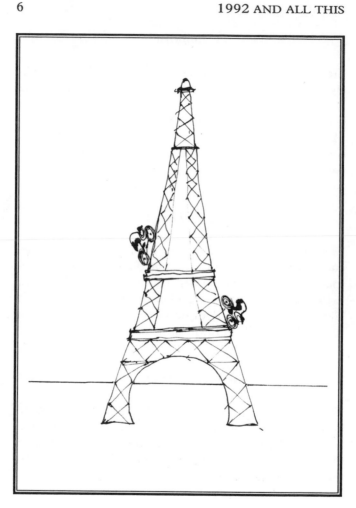

CYCLISME: THE TOUR D'EIFFEL

Sport

The French are keen sportsmen. They favour *le cyclisme* (see, of course, the famous Tour de France – or Tour de Force – and the shorter (but steeper) Tour d' Eiffel).

Horse racing – esp. the *Arc de Triomphe*, which is run round the centre of Paris.

French Cricket – played at Lourdes (although fashionable society also turns out for the monthly Paris Match).

Other decidedly French games: Boules or Jeu de Pommes (it was originally played with apples) and the insubstantial Jeu d'Esprit.

Culture (Fr. Couture)

The French Impressionists

A group of poor French artists who did impressions at a Parisian nightclub called the *Jolly Bargees* where almost anything was allowed. (It was the home of that licentious dance the 'You Can Can'.)

To begin with the Impressionists never had any money (Fr. *monet*) and often had to resort to eating grass (see Monet's – if not Manet's – *Déjeuner sur l' Herbe*). Later, however, they became more successful and ran a popular correspondence course to encourage the so-called Post-Impressionists.

The Impressionists introduced many new colours to their palettes: Sacre Bleu (Eng. *Sky Blue*), Carte Blanche

JEU DE POMMES

(*Paper White*), Jaune d'Arc (*Dark Yellow*) and Vigée Le Brun (*Very Brown*).

Memorable Impressionists:

* Monet (pron. Manet): painted water lilies (Fr. *Fleurs de l'eau*) in his sweetly scented garden at Givenchy.
* Degas: painted ballerinas and racehorses.
* Renoir: painted plump women before becoming a film director.
* Cézanne: painted innumerable pictures of Monsieur Victoire, his craggy-looking gardener.
* Mike Yarwood: doyen of popular impressionists and still around on the club circuit.
* Tooloose-Lautrec: so called because his diminutive stature meant that his suits were always too loose.
* Jean-Jacques Rousseau: naïvely he gave up a promising literary career (see *The Sentimental Elocution, Emile and the Detectives*, etc.) to concentrate on painting (together with some light Customs and Excise duty).

French Cuisine

The French are very proud of their cooking. They will eat anything (Fr. *Mange Tout*): frogs, snails, puppy dogs' tails. They even enjoy horseflesh, especially as a starter (Fr. *Horse d'Oeuvre*).

Often they smother their food in a rich sauce (Fr. *Oh la la!*) such as Hollandaise, Mayonnaise, Marseillaise (very stirring), Rabelaise (very saucy), or Crédit Lyonnaise (very rich).

LUNCHING ON GRASS BY MANET

It is little wonder that many Frenchmen get indigestion from eating too much rich, sweet food (Fr. *Pain au Chocolat*).

Recently the French have developed the so-called *Nouvelle Cuisine* (Eng. New Kitchen), a type of cooking that involves no food at all – so as not to dirty your smart new work surfaces, pots, pans, ovens, etc.

Napoleon

Napoleon Bonnypart tried to unite Europe under a French Empire. He himself, however, was not French but Corsican; and was, of course, rather coarse as a result.

He seized power with a 'whiff of grapefruit', urged on by his mistress, Madame de Pamplemousse. He then managed to confuse his enemies by claiming that 'an army marches on its stomach'. This was a fib. Napoleon always took the train. Many of his most famous battles were, as a result, fought at railway termini (Austerlitz, Waterloo, Trafalgar Square – now Charing Cross).

To show his respect for the memorable principles of the French Revolution – Liberty, Regality and Fraternity – Napoleon then felt free to put his various brothers on to the vacant thrones of Europe.

He was able to control this empire by sending his brothers secret messages in the famous Napoleonic Code (e.g. 'Able was I ere I saw Elba') which makes no sense whichever way you look at it.

Furthermore he reformed the Educational System, instituting the International Baccarat (compulsory card games for everyone up to the age of 18).

ALWAYS TOOK THE TRAIN

He himself soon become bored with cards. Often he would tell his wife (at very short notice), 'Not tonight, Josephat,' after she had gone to the trouble of organising an evening's Bridge (Fr. *Pont-et-une*).

Later Napoleon made the mistake of trying to invade Prussia (Eng. Russia) singlehandedly. (His other hand was tucked warmly into his coat lining.) He was thoroughly defeated and demoralised by Generals Janvier and Février (and, of course, by the harsh weather conditions), and had to catch the 18.12 back from Moscow.

He arrived home just in time to be met by the Duke of Wellington at Waterloo. And there he was memorably defeated once again.

Napoleon then (wisely) decided to retire altogether, living out his days with an elderly relative – Aunt Helena – somewhere in the Atlantic. This was a Good End to a Bad (but memorable) Thing.

FRENCH TEST PAPER

1. Expound obsessively upon the obsessive nature of French obsessions with special reference to *either* Zola's *Jacuzzi*, *or* Hugo's *The Lunchpack of Notre Dame*.
2. Of which famous picture did Cézanne remark, 'C'est magnifique mais ce n'est pas Degas'?
3. The Renault 5: innocent or guilty?
4. How many of the following could be certified as insane (Fr. *in Seine*)?

Budu?

Monsieur Raquin?

Simone de Bovary?

Pierrot le Fou?

5. Using *le régle du jeu* estimate the height of:
   (*a*) Mont Blanc;
   (*b*) Montmartre;
   (*c*) Mon Oncle.
6. Is Brittany more brittany than Normandy? Or *vice versa*?
7. Have you ever suffered from Aix en Provence?
8. 'Monte Carlo or Bust'. Discuss with glancing reference to both topless bathing *and* gambling on the French Riviera.
9. Who said 'Let them eat cake'?
   (*a*) Marie Anne Toilette?
   (*b*) Marcel Proust?
   (*c*) His mistress, Madeleine?
   (*d*) Monsieur Kipling?
   and was the cake referred to
   (*a*) One of the famous Gâteaux of the Loire? *or*
   (*b*) An éclair de la lune?

THE LOW COUNTRIES

BELGIUM

BELGIUM has always struggled to be memorable. Around the time of the First World War they introduced the slogan 'Remember Belgium', which enjoyed some success. But people soon discovered that they couldn't remember *why* they had remembered Belgium. And so they soon forgot about it again.

Belgium remains a Low Country with a low profile.*

Politics

The politics of Belgium are most uncertain. Nevertheless there definitely is – or was – a King of the Belgians. Memorably (but temporarily) he aborted his throne one afternoon in order to avoid having to gratify a bill legalising abdication which, as a Catholic, he was implacably deposed to.

Brussels (Belg. *Bruxelles*), the capital, is however, the centre of the EC. An attractive but quiet city, free from

---

* Some hysterical geographers, in an attempt to put Belgium on the map, have suggested that the Battle of Waterloo was actually fought there. Scholarly opinion, however, maintains that the famous victory was won either on a cricket pitch at Eton (nr. Windsor, Berks) or on the platform of a south London railway terminus.

huxelle and *buxelle*, Bureausels is tied up neatly but thoroughly with red tape so that nothing can happen there. There is, nevertheless, a discreet amount of spouting, sprouting, scouting, etc., during the long drawn-out political tussles (Belg. *tuxelles*) which constitute EC procedure.

Demography

The population of Belgium is divided very definitely (but not implacably) between those who speak Flemish (the Phlegms – or Belgians) and those who speak French (the Walloons – or Belgians).

The Flegms, although susceptible to the damp climate, tend to live in the low agricultural lands towards the sea, and are distrustful of the more sophisticated French-speaking town-dwellers (Belg. *'Brugge off!'*). They have chips on their shoulders – and, indeed, on everything else. They have mayonnaise on their chips.

The Woollens, on the other hand, are famous for the manufacture of walloon cloth – and also for their much malined lacework. If they do have a tendency to go on rather (Belg. Hot-air Walloons) they always remain perfect ghentlemen.

Famous Belgians

There are, famously, no famous Belgians. People may try to persuade you otherwise. Do not be taken in.

Plausible – but inadmissible – exceptions:

(*a*) Bicyclists. Painstaking research has shown that – with the possible exception of Daisy Daisy Imhalfcrazy (who was certainly *not* Belgian) – no cyclists are truly memorable. Not even Eddie Mercx.

(*b*) Tintin (and his dog, Rintintin) are cartoon characters and thus outside the scope of this discussion (Belg. *Banned Desinées*).

(*c*) Also excluded is Agatha L. Christie's famous, but fictional detective, Inspector Pierrot, with his melancholy white face and brilliant powers of reduction.

(*d*) The Angel of Mons, or Dame Edith Clavel (née Sitwell), was a saintly English nurse during the last war, and thus not Belgian at all.

Exports

Expensive beer, more expensive chocolates, Brussels sprouts.

National Characteristics

A marked tendency not to become memorable.

HOLLAND

Even lower than Belgium in world estimation is Holland, or the Netherlands (not to be confused with Nether-

netherland, which is altogether anotherland – and is, moreover, entirely imaginary).

Politics

Dutch political life, although presided over by a Queen (and possibly some Dykes and Dutchesses) is almost certainly bourgeois and unmentionable.

The Untied Nations do, however, hold (loosely) their supreme court at the Vague. Perhaps.

Water

The Dutch, living largely below sea-level, have become masters of water-control (Dutch: *Waterwirjks*). A series of dykes (invented by the brothers Anthony and Dick van Dyke), canals, clog-wheels and windmills has reclaimed vast tracts (D. *trechts*) of land from the sea (*zee*).

Whenever the water-level (*waterlüffel*) rises dangerously and the canals become swollen (*zwollen*) the Dutch can sound the alarm (*alaarm*), throw open the sluice gates (*slüys gaets*) and let the water flood out at Flushing before the dykes become overladen (*over Leyden*). Previously at moments of crisis the Dutch would either put their finger in a dyke or sit on their thumbs and wait and see (*wadensee*) what might happen.

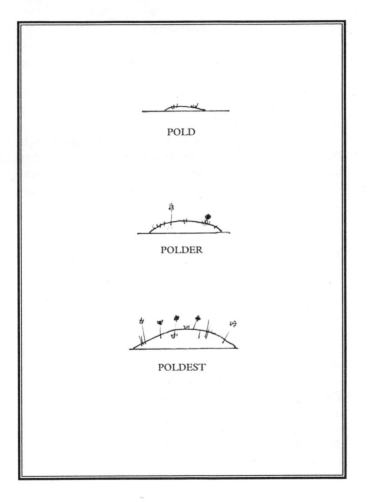

POLD

POLDER

POLDEST

STAGES OF LAND RECLAMATION

Economy

The Dutch economy is based on tulips, philips and large round cheeses.

Some Dutch industrial processes are, however, rather backward. Indeed Edam is actually *made* backwards (i.e. from right to left rather than from *lelft* to *rijt*).

Farming is not as advanced as might be expected. In Friesland they still only have black-and-white cows. And large-scale overproduction, coupled with closely enforced EC quotas, has led to the creation of a vast cider sea (*Zuyderzee*) in the North of the country.

Exports: Dutch auctions, dutch uncles, dutch caps, hamsters (from Hamsterdam).

Culture

Holland, perhaps surprisingly for such a low country, has always been in the vanguard of high culture. For centuries Dutch painting was dominated by a fleet of vans: Jan van Eyck, Roger van der Weyden, Hertz van Rental, Vincent van Gogh, Marco van Basten, etc. This represents more than just a thin vermeer of culture.

The Dutch invented still-life painting, specialising in the depiction of lavish spreads of food ('The Laughing Cauliflower' by Franz 'van' Hals, or numerous shellfish scenes by Ryp van Wynkle). The most famous Dutch food-painter was Rembrandt (who, in fact, changed his name from van Rijn so that it would be

PRIMITIVE AGRICULTURE

SAUCE OF INSPIRATION

more membrandtable). He used large quantities of
brown sauce on his canvases.

National Characteristics

Thrifty, liberal (sec esp. Amsterdamn, the Hookers of
Holland, legalised pottery – or Delftware), free-thinking,
clog-wearing, and with a strong lyking for bykes, dykes,
cheeses, etc.

LUXEMBURG

Luxemburg, which ought never to be confused with
Liechtenstein, is a tiny country renowned principally for
being a tiny country – and, possibly, a principality.

The economy of Luxemstein is largely (or tinily) invis-
ible, but it does have a famous Radio Station ('Radio
Liechtenburg') and a marked tendency to produce
postage stamps.

Together with Belgium and the Netherlands, Leic-
tralux forms the aptly named Benelux alignment which
hopes (with anylux) to promote trade and good-feeling
between the three countries. Thus Belhollich (as it is
sometimes called) is very definitely a Good Thing. Probably.

THE LOW COUNTRIES
TEST PAPER
—

1. Double Dutch is half as easy or twice as difficult as ordinary Dutch? Be decisive.
2. Should it be An twerp or A twerp? Be derisive.
3. Explain, if you can, the popularity of the Belgian soap-opera *Ostenders*.
4. 'You never get zutphen for nutphen.' Discuss this old Dutch proverb with reference to (*a*) Going Dutch (*b*) Dutch Auctions.
5. Would Dutch flower production be substantially increased if they moved from the cultivation of tulips to the propagation of threelips?
6. 'Ear we go! Ear we go! Ear we go!' Is this a just reflection upon the life of Vincent van Gogh? Be incisive.
7. Estimate in either flemish or guilders (but not both) the literary worth of:
    (*a*) *The Moon's a Walloon*;
    (*b*) *Le Bruges et le Noir*;
    (*c*) *Kursaal Gummidge*.
8. Does Pop Culture owe more to Roy Luxemburg or Radio Liechtenstein? Be snappy.
9. Would you know Gouda from Edam? Be truthful.

SCANDINAVIA

FEW countries have so much geography as those of Scandinavia. Glaciers, geysers, saunas, lakes, fjords, fjelds, morasses, terminal moraines, Russian sub-moraines, hydro-ecletic dams: all of them are here. Or, rather, there.

There are three countries very definitely in Scandinavia – Sweden, Norway and Denmark. And two that are only potentially Scandinavian – Iceland and Finland. Jutland and Lappland have achieved notoriety but not yet any definite geographical location.

SWEDEN

Statistically speaking (as one does 32% of the time) Sweden can lay claim to most (63%) of the memorable European statistics. Sweden has:

- the highest per capita income in Europe;
- the highest suicide rate;
- the largest number of alcholics;
- the greatest incidence of ABBA recordings;
- the most Swedes;
- the least turnips, mangelwurzels, neeps, etc.

Economy

Sweden's flourishing economy is built of several pillars:

(*a*) *Rich Natural Resources*: iron and/ore timber (pine, fur, birch twigs, etc.), woodrow electric power, ABBA records.

(*b*) *Well-Managed Industries*: Volvo, Saab, Primus stoves, safety matches, crispbread bakeries, massage parlours, etc.

(*c*) *Cheap Power*: hydro electricity (damns), geysers (blasts), natural gas (controlled by the Smörgåsbord), Primus stoves, safety matches.

Exports: ABBA, Saabba, sauna, Swedish au pairs (esp. from the north of the country – cf. Norrland Nannies).

Imports: Russian submarines.

Agriculture

Crispwheat (for crispbread) and stringbeans (Sw. Strindbergs), especially upp in the upplands round Uppsala. Also cattle (kept in stockholms) and goats from Gotenburg. And, of course, swedes are cultivated (up to a point) all over.

Politics

Sweden has always tended to be neutral, favouring beige colours, blond woods and *écru* soft-furnishings.

The Swedes have become the arbiters of World Merit.

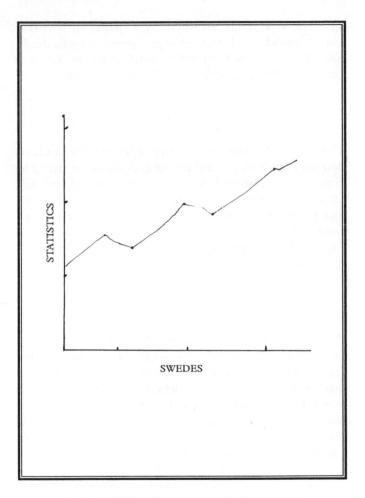

GRAPH SHOWING THE RISE IN THE NUMBER OF
STATISTICS (PER CAPITA) IN SWEDEN

The Noble Prize is awarded by a panel of Swedish nobles (*nobels*) – Kings (*Kongs*), peers (*gynt*s), lords (*ljords*), etc. – for outstanding proficiency in Science, Literature, Peas, Strindbergs, RE, Geoggers, etc.

Tennis

The affluent Swedes have plenty of leisure time and, so that they don't sit around moping, drinking or trying to improve the National Statistics, the Government has introduced compulsory tennis with considerable success. Sweden has produced several notable champions: Bjorn Borg (who later went on to form the middle bit of ABBA), Stefan Eggnog, Mats Wilhander, Bats Backhander, Fitz Forhander.

Culture

For many years the memorable Swedish Film Industry has been presided over by the famous husband-and-wife team of Ingmar and Ingrid Bergman. Together they have made a string of notoriously depressing nature documentaries about Swedish flora and fauna (Sw. *søra und sauna*), including the classics – *Autumn Cantata, Wild Strawberries, The Seventh Seal, Notorious, Bjorn Free, My Life as a Log*, etc. Sweden also leads the way in the production of training films for the medical professions (see such seminal titles as *Swedish Dentists On Heat, Naughty Nurses Go Loco, Lady Doctor!, The Pedal-operated Tooth Drill: A User's Guide, Saucy Sauna Spankerama*).

THE SEVENTH SEAL – AND OTHER FILMS
OF A DEPRESSING NATURE

Notional Characteristics

Fair-haired, blue-eyed, a tendency to fall silent and sink into depression, a tendency to drink too much, a tendency to become overexcited – to sing and dance and extemporise poetry – a tendency to fall silent again.

NORWAY

Norway is in many respects the same as Sweden, although less so economically and statistically, and more so geographically.

Norway is particularly rich in glaciers, geysers, fjords, fjelds, waterfjalls, etc.

Economy

Wood. Norway is very densely wooded, especially with the indigenous Norwegian pine (or Christmas Tree, as it is called, after the famous Norwegian – or probably Danish – writer Hans Christmas Andersen) and the rather smarter Spruce tree.

The popular jingle put out by the Norwegian Lumber Board (and later covered by the Beatles), 'Norwegian Wood – isn't it good?', created a vogue for striped pine kitchens in the 1960s. Now, however, the forests of Norway are being stripped before they ever reach the kitchen due to a plague of acid drops left by British litter louts ('The Dirty Men of Europe').

THE STRIPED PINE

Industries: See Wood, but also trawling (N. *trolling*) for sardines, roll-mops, pilchards, trolls, etc.

Exports: Thor Heyerdahl, striped pine trees, trolls, roll-mops, troll-mops, etc.

Imports: Acid rain drops.

Oslo, the capital city, is a thriving town with its famous illuminated esplanade (The Northern Lights or *Adora Bordialles*) and late-edition evening paper called the *Midnight Sun*.

Politics

Fiercely democratic, patriotic, etc., with a great distrust of chiselling, quisling, embezzling, viking and other underhand behaviour.

National Characteristics

A tendency to be like the Swedes (though not as good at tennis).

DENMARK (or perhaps Jutland)

Compared to its Scandinavian neighbours Denmark has remarkably few geographical features. It is very flat (see also Low Countries). This, however, does not prevent the Danes from being thoroughly Scandinavian (fair-eyed, blue-haired, Faer-isled, etc.) in all other respects.

A SAD TALE

One of the most memorable depressives of all time was indeed a Dane: Hamlet, or the Prince of Denmark. A full account of his brief but sad life can be found in Shakespeare's play 'To Be Or Not To Be'. Hamlet (D. *Bacon omelet*), haunted by his father's ghost and crossed in love by his mad sweetheart Elsie-Nora, tries to do away with himself just behind Arras ('The slings and Arras of contagious fortune . . .' etc). Meanwhile Jorrocks, the dead jester, tells some very old jokes. They die too. As does everyone else. It is a very grave tale.

Economy

The Danish economy is fuelled (D. *Diesel*) by exports: Great Danes, Danish pastries, bacon hamlets, blue cheeses, blue movies (D. *Fünen games*), lager (probably).

Copenhagen, the principal city, is memorably 'Wonderfulwonderful'. Quite why it is so 'Wonderfulwonderful' is less clear. But there it is. Also there (in the harbour) is a famous (and, very probably, wonderfulwonderful) statue of 'The Little Barmaid', erected in memory of the Great Dane-ish (if not Norwegian) writer and drinker Hands Xmas Andersen.

SCANDINAVIAN CULTURAL GIANTS

Scandinavian Culture is dominated by the towering figures Ibsen, Kierkegaard and August Stringvest.

Kierkergrad was a Danish (or, possibly, Swedish) philosopher who invented the multiple-choice question

THE LITTLE BARMAID

in his book *Either, Or*. Later, however, he became obsessively worried about his house burning down, and so invented *Angst* (Eng. obsessive worry) and the fireguard (D. *firgaard*).

August Shingaard was a Swedish (or, conceivably, Danish) playwright who shocked the literary world by running off with his governess, Miss Julie.

The bewhiskered dramatist Henry Inkpen was almost certainly Norwegian. His many plays include *The Wild Duck* (later filmed by the Bergmans as *The Wild Gooseberry*), *The Pillars of Propriety*, *An Enemy of the Steeple* (or *The Master Builder*) and *Hedda Gabbler*, the tragic tale of a garrulous housewife in a small town.

PROBABLE, POSSIBLE OR PLAUSIBLE SCANDINAVIAN COUNTRIES

Iceland

Iceland (Ic. *Island*) is a small island (Ic. *Iceland*) in the North Sea made up in almost equal parts of ice and land.

Its economy is based entirely on fishing (cod) and oil (cod liver) which makes it very economical to run.

Exports: Magnus Magnusson.

Finland

Finland represents the northern end of Europe. Its people, as a result, are known as the Finnish.

THE VIKINGS

The Scandinavians (Old Norse *Vikings*) tried briefly to bring Europe under their own sway (ON *swein*) in the early Muddle Ages.

The vikings were fearsome warriors with long hair, long beards, long horns on their helmets (or perhaps not), long swords, long johns, etc. And they made very short shrift of those who stood (or sat) in their way.

Viking (Eng. fighting) is a particularly brutish form of warmongering, involving rape, pillage, spillage, roughage and toughage. And the Vikings, having invented it, were particularly good at it. Thus they threatened to become Top Nation.

But the expense of carrying on all these overseas campaigns soon became too great for them. So they introduced the Danegeld. Large sums of Danegeld had to be paid up by the unfortunate (and unready) Angles, Saxons, Jutes, etc., to finance the viking raids upon their lands.

This method of invasion on the instalment plan worked well with the English who, to their credit, have always favoured the Higher Purchase, but rather less well elsewhere.

Moreover the vikings (Eng. Saga Louts), having very little culture (except for lager), rapidly became dissimilated wherever they settled and started being called Norman instead of Swein Forkbreath and Ragnar Logbook.

And thus the Viking attempt to unify Europe failed – which was almost certainly a Good Thing.

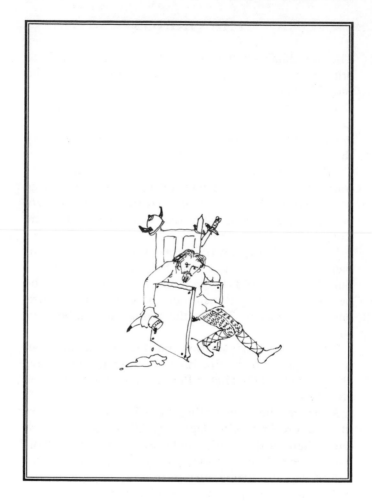

VIKING CULTURE

SCANDINAVIAN TEST PAPER

PART I

1. The recent success of Scandinavian tennis is only the tip of the:
   (*a*) Iceborg?
   (*b*) Edberg?
   (*c*) Carlsberg?
   Be serious (if you can).
2. Phonetically speaking would you rather 'lunch' with 'Munch' or 'look' at 'Moonk'?
3. To what extent can Norway be termed 'the doorway to the North'?
   (*a*) No way?
   (*b*) Half-way?
   (*c*) Ask a doorwegian?
4. Would you rather be obese or odense?
5. Assess Grieg's strengths as *either* a piano stylist *or* an England cricket captain. Be fair.
6. 'To be or not to be.' What is the answer?
7. Give the pH value of Acid Reindeer.
8. The bestselling Scandinavian car is:
   (*a*) the Volvo Estate?
   (*b*) the Saab Convertible?
   (*c*) the Fjord Escort?

PART II

9. 'The Viking warrior was a tough knut to crack.' Consider this verdict with special reference to Eric Bloodbath, Harald Hardrada, and Harald Softrada.
10. 'Saturday night's all right for viking.' Translate into *either* runes *or* Norse Code.
11. The Viking idea of heaven was:
    (*a*) Valhalla?
    (*b*) Valpolicella?
    (*c*) Twelve pints of lager and a packet of crisps?
12. Should the vexed authorship of *A Rune of One's Own* be ascribed to Beo Woolf or to his sister Virginia?

ITALY

ITALY is, geographically speaking, the most memorable country in Europe, being shaped like a boot. No other country in the world starts with such a natural advantage (not even Bhutan which, despite its name, is shaped like a crumpled paper handkerchief). Italy, however, has not rested there.

She has also gone on to become the cradle of European Civilisation (The Grandeur That Was Rome, the Agony and the Ecstasy that was the Renaissance, and the other thing that was the Baroque).

Perhaps because of these successes Italy has failed rather badly to become politically or economically memorable. Nevertheless set out below are the very few facts that can be recalled.

Politics

Since Mussolini (*The Deuce*) there have been no memorable Italian politicians which, all things considered, is probably a good thing – except perhaps for rail passengers (see Trains).

The Government now is nearly always confused and weak, and tends to change weekly which only adds to the confusion.

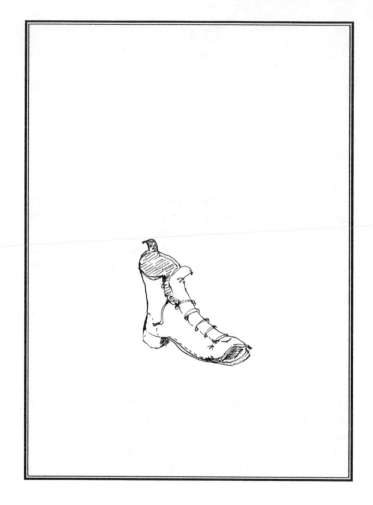

DISTINCTIVE SHAPE

There are several parties (all equally weak) which should not be confused:

The Christian Democrats, or socialites
The Communists, or socialists
The Socialists, or ageing liberals
The Progressives, or ageing porn queens
The Bring-a-bottle, or complete *fiasca*.

Because of the weakly changes in government real political power is confined elsewhere. It is in the hands of:

The Mafia – an honourable society of Sicilian mutes with widespread interests in both the construction and destruction businesses;
The Masons – a secret brotherhood of businessmen, bankers and jellies with widespread interests in business, banking and jelly (see also Gelati);
The Madonna* – the Mother of God,† with widespread interest in the poor, the weak and the confused (see the Italian Government).

Economy

Most of the Italian economy is black. And if it is too dark for even the Tax Inspectors to see, it is obviously too obscure for a general book of this sort.

---

* Not to be confused with either Madonna, who only *felt* like a virgin, or Maradona, who not only felt like a virgin but did something about it (see Paternity Suit).

† Not to be confused with the Hand of God (see Maradona).

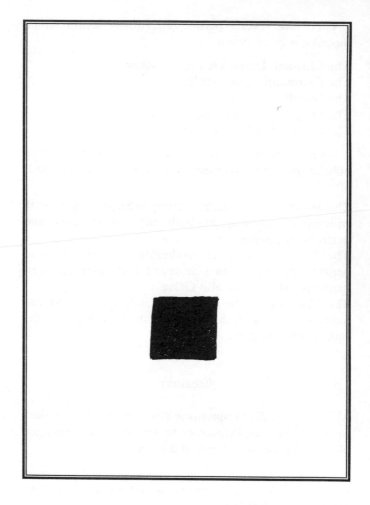

AN OVERVIEW OF THE ITALIAN ECONOMY

'There is, however, one memorable and significant fact about the Italian economy: the North of the Country is rich and industrial, while the South is poor and given over to the cultivation of Italian Plum Tomatoes.

Italians, however, are unable to agree on where the North ends and the South begins. Some (the Milanese) set the dividing line just south of Milan, others (the Florentines) place it below Florence, while the Romans insist that the boundary lies fractionally south of Rome. No one can understand what the Neapolitans say on the subject so they are generally assumed to live in the South.

In a further effort to confuse the Neapolitans into admitting this fact, Southern Italy is sometimes called *Il Mezzogiorno* (The Afternoon). No one in Naples, of course, knows what this word means (see-esta).

Industries: Never in the afternoon (see-esta again), Fiat motor cars, Olivetti typewriters (see *Tippa alla Fiorentina*), Gelati* (or ice cream).

Exports: Fashion (Armani jackets, Moschino frocks, Ferragamo shoes, cement overcoats), Italian Plum Tomatoes, pasta (spaghetti, macaroni, tagliatelli, mastroianni, vermicelli, pasolini, zeffirelli, etc.), organised crime, small plaster statuettes of Michelangelo's *David*, 'Ciao'.

Imports: Tourists, footballers.[†]

---

* Not to be confused with Gelli (for jelly turn to P2, not to be confused with page 2), or indeed with any of the other famous Italian puddings: *Il Dolce* (Mussolini), *crema* (custard), *custardo* (cream), *zuppa inglese* (a trifle confusing). As the Italians so rightly say, 'La dolce fa niente.' ('There's nothing like pudding' or 'Mussolini never did anything').

[†] Everyone in Italy is football mad or, as they say, 'Cosi fan tutti'.

Transport

Since the demise of Il Dolce the trains memorably no longer run on time. Many of them no longer run at all. You should, however, be aware that there are several different types of train, some very much less fast than others:

Il Expresso: stops at every station (for a small black coffee)

Il Rapido: stops in between every station (for no very good reason)

Il Rapidissimo: stops very suddenly between every station

Il Diretto: stops directly it leaves the first station

Il Locale: never starts.

Other traditional modes of Italian transport include: the gondolas of Venice, the planes of Lombardy, vespers (mopeds for priests, popes, cardinals, etc.), and omnibuses (see J. Caesar, sickness of).

National Characteristics

Jovial, prone to song, moustachioed, emotional, prone to argument, childlike, not brave, reckless behind the wheel of a car (*Fiat al dente*), prone in the afternoon (See-esta yet again).

Culture

Italy has more culture than any other country in Europe. Almost every town has both a picture gallery (It. *pinacolada*) and a medieval (though later restored) cathedral (It. *duomo*), often with a *duomo* (Eng. dome) and accompanying bell-tower (It. *bellavista*).

It was the Italians who memorably (and generously) invented the Renaissance (It. *Risorgimento*), finally sorting out the Muddle Ages and rediscovering the Classical Arts of bronze-casting, shot-putting, *al fresco* painting (or giotting things down on walls), and double-entry bookkeeping.

Renaissance Men

These masters were easily distinguishable (and very distinguished) because they were exceptionally (and equally) good at everything (or anything).

Michelangelo: sculptor and plumber; he carved the very notable statue of David as well as installing the elaborate flush-operated water-tank in the Pope's private Cistern Chapel.

Botticelli: painter and astronomer; having produced a striking portrait of his first wife, Vera, dressed as a flower-girl, he discovered Venus.

Leonardo da Vinci: artist and engineer; after painting the most memorable picture in the world, the *Mona Lisa* (or *The Anaconda's Smile*) he devoted himself to inventing aeroplanes, motorcars (the *Fiat Quattrocento*), electric toothbrushes, etc.*

Garibaldi: soldier and baker; one of the heroes of the *Rinascimento*, Gary Baldy, together with his band of red-coats (the Red Brigade), introduced the famous 'squashed-fly' biscuit into Italy, supplanting the over-priced, chocolate-filled Bourbon regime.

Note: High seriousness of Italian Art. Although the Italians are light-hearted in most other things they do take culture seriously. Their few attempts at 'humorous art' have not been successful.

- *Leonardo's Cartoon* is memorably unamusing; he forgot the caption. (It was his one failure.)
- Dante's *Divine Comedy* is very short on laughs for such an infernally long book.
- MacHiavelli's *The Little Prince*, although a charming and whimsical parable, was mistaken by the critics for a tract on political amorality, thus earning its author (an Italian-born Scotsman) a damnably low reputation.

THE GRANDEUR THAT WAS ROME

The Ancient Romans, who to some extent must be considered Italians (although, of course, it remains unclear whether they were Northern or Southern Italians) were the first people to try and unify Europe. This was called the Roman Empire.

* Alas all these inventions were curiously obsolete as no one knew how to fly, drive, brush their teeth, etc.

COULDN'T THINK OF A CAPTION

It was a great success and a Good Thing – for a while.
At one time it stretched from Spain to Turkey, or from
Britain to Morocco – or, rather, both.

The Aims of the Empire

The Romans were very concerned to raise standards in
the countries they conquered. The standard was usually
surmounted with a Beagle and the Roman motto, SPQR
(Small Profits, Quick Returns). Behind the standard
would be arranged a massive army (or Legion), divided
in cohorts (or Cohorts). So organised were the Romans
that the cohorts were further divided into Maniples,
Scruples and, even, Wimples. (These last two were,
respectively, for conscientious objectors and cowards.)

At moments of crisis the soldiers would either shout
'Pax Romana' and all the fighting would cease until the
same time the next day, or they would disguise themselves as a tortoise. This ploy may have slowed them
down but it often gave them the advantage of surprise.
As a result the Romans (Italians) very soon became Top
Nation.

Benefits of Romanisation

The Romans conferred many benefits on the lands they
overcame. They brought a high degree of almost geomet-
ric organisation. Julius Caesar divided Gaul into three
parts, having previously left winter quarters himself.

RAISING STANDARDS

They built roads (Ancient British, *woads*), which were straight and led, without exception, to Rome.

They also established Roman Baths wherever they went, even in such chilly countries as Britain (England). Many English place-names still bear witness to the invaders' obsession with personal cleanliness (*Bath*, *Basin*gstoke, Water*loo*, etc.).

The Romans instituted great building projects to add lustre to their Empire and to entertain the plebeians during their frequent Roman holidays (Hadrian's Wall, the Pont du Gard, the Gare du Nord, the Coliseum, the Hippodrome, the Odéon, the Curzon, etc.).

The Emperors

The Roman Empire was memorably governed by a succession of Emperors:

J. Caesar: a keen squash-player who suffered from travel sickness. Having been told expressly to watch out for the Tides of March he was, unsurprisingly, surprised by a group of very un-tidelike conspirators (Cato, Cicero, Catiline, Cassius, etc.) and done to death. What with his great surprise, he could only come up with the rather blunt (but none the less memorable) last line, 'Et tu Brute' ('Oh you brutes').

Augustus: so called because he was so august (or vice versa).

Nero: perhaps the most corrupt of all Roman Emperors; he was still fiddling even while Rome burnt. Later he

FOND OF BATHS

STABLE GOVERNMENT

became depressed at his lack of success as a poet and insurance fiddler, and committed suicide. His last words, 'Qualis artifex pereo' ('How very artificial it all seems now'), are a fine example of Roman camp (*castrum*).

Caligula: although thoroughly unstable he ruled jointly with his horse.

I Claudius: had a terrible stammer and a no less terrible resemblance to Derek Jacobi. He was poisoned by his wife, uttering the memorable last words 'So, Goodbye To All That'. (See Robert Graves's brilliant account of his life, *Agrippina, Penny Puce*.)

Hadrian: best known as a builder. He later retired to a villa in the hills outside Rome, telling his subjects, 'Et in Arcadia ego' ('I too have a place in the country').

After this the emperors became less and less memorable and found themselves swept inexorably into Gibbon's *Decline and Fall of the Roman Empire*. This was a Bad Thing, especially for the Roman Empire.

Causes of the Decline and Fall of the Roman Empire

(*a*) Gibbon's enormous erudition.
(*b*) Waves of barbarians (Ostrogoths, Visigoths, Disigoths, Fisigoths, Huns, Vandals and Lager Louts) blazed into the Empire from Eastern Europe. With their light cavalry they were able to outmanoeuvre the Roman tortoise and set fire to the capital (*capitol*).

IT KILLED THE ANCIENT ROMANS . . .

(c) The Roman plebs demanded even more holidays and places of entertainment (the Palladium, the Circus Maximus, the ABC Fulham Road, etc.).

(d) Many of the Romans became too ancient and were killed off by the difficulty of learning Latin.

ITALIAN TEST PAPER

PART I

1. How do you like your spaghetti cooked?
    (a) Al dente?
    (b) Al fresco?
    (c) Al Jolson?
2. Assess the mineral value of:
    (a) Carrara Marble;
    (b) Irving Stone;
    (c) The Baroque.
    Be adamant.
3. To what extent can the traffic problems in central Rome be set down to *La donna e mobile*?
4. How long might it take to travel by Rapido between the stations of Sottopassagio and Uscita? (Be prepared for long delays.)
5. Estimate the full impact of the young Sophia Loren upon our conception of *bella figura*.
6. Compute the cultural value of:
    (a) Just one Cornetto;
    (b) P2;
    (c) Quattro Stagione (with extra mozzarella);
    (d) Settebello.

7. Does Fellini's film *Il Duce Vita* give an over-glamorous account of Mussolini's early years?

8. Would you expect to find the Brancacci Chapel:
   - (*a*) in Rome?
   - (*b*) in Florence?
   - (*c*) in Restauro?

PART II

9. What time was it exactly when Cicero exclaimed 'O Tempora, O Mores'? (Answers should be computed to the nearest twenty minutes.)

10. Measure the altitude of:
    - (*a*) The Tarpeian Rock;
    - (*b*) Up Pompeii;
    - (*c*) Caesar's wife;
    - (*d*) The heights of infamy.

11. Were the Carthaginians:
    - (*a*) Hannibal?
    - (*b*) Vegetabal?
    - (*c*) Mineral?

    Be sensibal.

12. If it came to the pinch would you rather have bread *or* circuses? Be honest.

13. Make out a case for the Vocative.

14. Who wrought more havoc, iron, etc.?
    - (*a*) Attila the Hun?
    - (*b*) Alaric the Goth?
    - (*c*) Asterix the Gaul?
    - (*d*) Winnie the Pooh?

    Write on one side of the *tabula* only.

SPAIN

SPAIN (and hence Portugal) are the most southerly countries in Europe. This to some extent might account for the Spaniards' (if not the Portuguese's) hot blood, hot sausages, hot weather, (¿) hot-water bottles (?), etc.

Basic Geometry

Spain has the rare – and decidedly ungeographical – decency to be entirely square. The Spaniards, moreover, have compounded this natural advantage by placing their capital, Madrid, exactly (and deliberately) in the middle. (¡Well done!)

For the rest, Spinach geography is altogether less memorable. There are, nevertheless, some rivers (see the Ebro, Douro, Tagus, Bogus, etc.) and, more especially, mountains (see-erras of various descriptions) that are not entirely without point (Sp. *Picos di Europas*).

National Characteristics

The Spanish are proud (Sp. *Aragonese*) and proud of it – except, of course, for the Oranges, which are servile, and the Brusques, who are apt to be rather basque.

A SERVILE ORANGE

Even in the Middle Ages the Spanish were under the delusion (Sp. *Andalusian*) that they were terribly grand. Spain was famous for its clean-living aristocrats, the so-called Knights of Castile. A wave of proud and legendary heroes, such as Tel Cid, Sir Vantes, Olé King Colé and, of course, Sir Don Quixote, drove the Moors, giants, windmills, etc., out of Spain. Moor or less.

Politics

After the long reign (mainly on the plane) of the fascist dictatador, General Franco (who had established a strict Mañana Republic following the deplorable Spanish-Seville War), Spain has been restored to democratic monarchy. And a good thing too – especially for King One Carlos and, indeed, for everyone else now jostling in the corridors (Sp. *corridas*) of power.

Economy

Tourism is the mainstay of the Spanish economy. Every year millions of British holidaymakers pack their bags, and take a Package Tour to the Costa Packet. The beaches are, of course, packed.

Exports: Steps (to Italy), Riding Schools (to Austria), flies, omelettes and onions.

A PACKAGE HOLIDAY

Culture

The Spanish have developed a very distinct (and distinct-
ly colourful) culture based on Bull-fights, Flamenco
(Eng. Tapas dancing) and Pelota (Eng. Basquethall).

They also boast a rich artistic tradition. The Old Spanish Masters – Velazquez (painter of the long-delayed mas-
terpiece *Las Mañanas*), Murillo y Goya – were content to
stay in Spain and exhibit their work at the Prado. But
later Spanish artists (Pueblo Picasso, Hello Dali, Isam-
bard Kingdom Buñuel, etc.) felt compelled to rush off to
Paris and hang out on the Rive Gauche, feeling blue (for
brief periods), surreally really weird, cuboid, gauche, etc.
As a result many of their best works are now housed in
Paris in the incredible collection of the Count d'Orsay.

Spain and Europe

Having discovered America, the New World, the spheri-
cal nature of the globe, etc. (see 1492 and all that), Spain
decided to acquire a European Empire.

Consequently, Carlos I of Spain became Charles V of
the Wholly Roman (but now partly Spanish) Empire and
founded a Hapsburg Dynasty* with wide- (and thin-)
spread possessions in the Netherlands.

Note. This Hapsburg Dynasty should not, whenever possible, be
confused with the Habspurg Dynasty which presided over the Austro-
Bulgarian Empire. This latter Dynasty, although possessing the same
distinctive jaw and, indeed, name, is quite distinct – and comes later
(page 88).

Charles's son, Philip II of Spain (but Philip I of the
Roly Human Empire), showed a keen appreciation of
Spain's unparalleled geometrical amenities. It was he
who built (along rigorously straight and parallel lines) the
memorable royal palace called El Equilateral.

The Counter Defamation

At about this time Martin Luther nailed his Ph.D. thesis
to a door in Battenburg. He then proceeded to protest
loudly about the self-indulgence of the Popes; the incom-
prehensibility of Roman Catholic church services; smells
and bells; the lack of good hymn tunes; the price of nails;
and the diet of worms he was obliged to subsist on.

Philip II, being staunchly Roman Catholic (as well as
Wholly Roman Emperor), was not amused. He launched
the Counter Defamation and proceeded to protest loudly about the awfulness of Martin Luther, the tunelessness
of *his* hymns, the depravity of his eating habits, etc.

The Spanish Disquisition – under the memorable Tor-
turemada – were (perhaps unexpectedly) important
agents of this Counter Deformation. They ruthlessly
rooted out offenders by asking them 'What's the answer?'
without even telling them what the question was. And
then torturing them if they failed to reply correctly. This
was called the Inconsequential Method and was a Bad
Thing.

DISGUSTING TABLE MANNERS

The Decline of Spain

In the end Spain's attempts to dominate the whole of Europe failed for three very good reasons:

1. The Spanish Amontillado (flying the Jolly Rioja) was fairly and squarely beaten by Sir Francis Drake and his drum. (Good show! Plymouth Ho! Yo ho ho! etc.)
2. The Netherlands became too revolting. (Rotters! Damn! Blast!)
3. The War of the Spanish Concession resulted in Spain having to concede most of her possessions. (Gib, Gib, Gib Hooray!)

PORTUGAL

PORTUGAL, 'our oldest ally', while not exactly Spanish (being very definitely Portuguese) is invariably considered in the same breath as Spain. It is part of the same Hibernian Penninsula.

Historical Background

Portugal (like Britain) is a maritime nation. Its most famous men are sailors: Henry the Navigator, Tabasco da Gamba and Magellyfish (the original Portuguese Man of War). On most of their voyages, however, these national heroes headed determinedly away from Europe, beyond the limits of knowledge and, hence, the scope of this book.

Politics

Despite occasional revolutions, earthquakes, dictators, etc., Portugal is a demographic republic.

Economy

Portugal has an unsophisticated, agricultural economy based on garlic, onions and cintrus fruits from the groves around Citra.

Exports: Port from the port of Porto (Port. *Oporto*) and extra Madeira (Port. *Estramadura*) from the Ilha da Madeira.

Culture

Over the years Portuguese art (such as it is) has gone almost completely to pot.

IBERIAN TEST PAPER

1. If you went to a bullfight would you be surprised to see:
   (*a*) Matadors?
   (*b*) Picadors?
   (*c*) Dianadors?
2. Write anything you know about any (or all) of the following long-term residents on the Costa del Crime: El Sid, Solly Sombra, Terry (Sp. *Terez*) Towelling. (Put in an envelope and send to the Serious Crime Squad, Scotland Yard, London SW1.)
3. Would you expect to start a Spanish meal with:
   (*a*) Gazpatchio?
   (*b*) Lobster Basque Soup?
   (*c*) Mañana Custard?
4. Guess the nationality of *either* El Greco *or* General Franco. Be careful.
5. If you had to get from Alicante to Zaragoza in a hurry would you travel by:

    (*a*) Mule?

    (*b*) Plane (weather permitting)?

    (*c*) Auto da Fe?

6. After the bull is killed by the matador is it made into beefburgos?

7. In your considered opinion is Gaudi's *Sangria Familia* cathedral at Barcelona:

    (*a*) Too gaudy?

    (*b*) Not gaudy enough?

    (*c*) Almost indistinguishable from a Canaletto?

8. 'Calderon's later plays are little more than pot-boilers.' Discuss with reference to anything you know.

9. Explain (in English but not Portuguese) the rules of *either* Faro *or* Setuball.

10. Using your skill and judgement arrange in order of size the following Balearic Islands: Ibiza, Majolica, Minerva, Alderney and Sark.

SWITZERLAND

SWITZERLAND is a small country set among the Alps in the centre of Europe. Happily (and efficiently), it is populated by small people – the gnomes of Zürich – and is thus very successful.

Political neutrality and financial know-how (i.e. discreet banking by numbered accountants) have made Switzerland into the hub of Europe.

Its dramatic alpine scenery has appeared bristling *on* many a chocolate box, and its dramatic dairy-rich chocolates have appeared nestlé-ing *in* many a chocolate box.

Political Character

Switzerland (Sw. *Crampon Helvetia*) is divided into many independent crampons (Sw. *cantons*), each with its own cultural and political traditions. It should be noted that, rather than speaking Swiss, the Swiss speak German, French, Cantonese, Italian and Romansh. And it is necessary to take a very stringent exam in all these relevant languages in order to get a Swiss passport (or Great St Bernard Pass).

The Swiss have, over the centuries, learnt the art of tolerating each other. It was not always so. Calvin was very intolerable. As was William Tell (Eng. Will Scarlet), a very red and very cross bowman who could not abide

A SMALL NATION

A VERY CROSS BOWMAN

apples (Sw. *appenzell*) and would shoot them on sight (on head, on the smallest provocation, etc.).

However, the Swiss then instituted the International Red Cross to try and calm cross (and red) people down and give them medical attention. It has been a great success, and is now firmly established at Geneva (*Sw/It. Genoa*) on the shores of Lake Genova (Sw/Sc. *Lac Lomond*).

National Character

The Swiss are notoriously punctual and are clean to the point of fanaticism. Before entering the country they always wipe their feet on the mat (Sw. *Zermatt*).

Industry

Switzerland has no natural resources, apart from milk. They rely therefore on high-quality manufacturing industries, making milk, chocolates, milk chocolates and, of course, cuckoo clocks.

Imports: coals (to Neuchatel), tourists and chalet girls.

Exports: Guards (to the Vatican) and chocolate cuckoo clocks.

SWISS CULTURE

Sports

The Swiss are very keen on all Winter Sports (Sw. *Interlarkenabout*). They even invented the so-called Cresta Run (or Swiss Roll) at St Moritz (Sw/Fr. *St Tropez*) to amuse the many tourists.

Culture

Swiss culture memorably consists of the cuckoo clock – and very little else.

SWISS TEST PAPER

1. 'Better red than cross.' Discuss this adage with reference to William Tell and the virtues of neutrality.
2. Can you hum the tune to *either* 'Oh Dear What Can the Matterhorn' or 'By the Bonnie, Bonnie Banks of Loch Leman'? Well, don't.
3. Does Swiss culture owe its poor reputation to:
   (*a*) Harry Lime?
   (*b*) Basel Brush?
   (*c*) Calvin (and/or Hobbes)?
4. Assess exhaustively the varying importance of lacework, fretwork, clockwork and hardwork to the development of Swiss manufacturing industry.
5. Is the Jungfrau:
   (*a*) Jung's wife?
   (*b*) The Swiss name for Mont Blanc?

    (c) The Swiss name for Blanc Mange?

    (d) None (or all) of the above?

6. Can you name any anonymous Swiss bankers? Be discreet.

7. If you heard the first cuckoo clock of spring would you write to *The Times*? And what would you write?

8. How do you cook *Lausanne Verdi*?

GERMANY

A LTHOUGH ruthlessly efficient in most things, Germany is geographically confused. It is always altering its borders with little (or no) consideration for natural boundaries, racial demography or, indeed, the general reader.

After the Second World War, Germany was divided memorably into two parts – West Germany (GBH) and East Germany (FDR) – separated by the Berlin Wall, Iron Curtain, Veil of Tears, etc. Now, however, they have had the decorators (Kohlfax und Fowler) in. The curtains have been changed and the wall knocked down to give an open-plan, all-in-one Modern Germany. This is a Good Thing. Or a Bad Thing. (Depending on your view of things German, the strength of the Deutschmark, the sanity of Nicholas Ridley, etc.).

It is, however, at the time of writing (10.30 a.m.), too early for anyone to pronounce with authority on the subject. Besides, East Germany (UDI) has for so many years been obscured from view by walls, curtains and veils that no one can remember anything very much about it. Nearly all the memorable facts gathered below are, therefore, West German in origin.

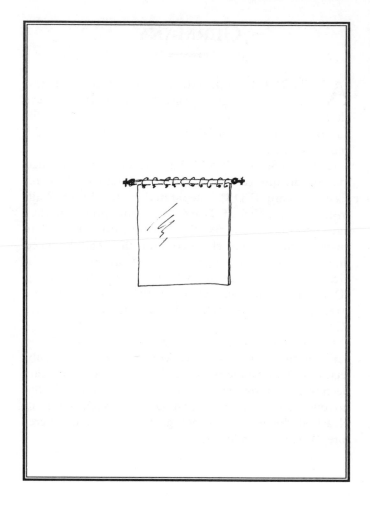

THE IRON CURTAIN

Physical Characteristics

There is only one truly memorable German river, the Rhine (or Ruhr). It is a ruthlessly industrial waterway* famous for its toll-castles, mineral resources (coal, rhinestones, rhine gold) and manufacturing plants (steelworks, car factories, chemical labs (esp. Faben & Faben), Mainz electricity, etc.

Industry

The German motor industry leads Europe: BMW, VW, Mercedez Bends, Opel and Audi. As they so rightly say,. '*Vorsprung durch technik*' (Eng. the suspension is technically very good).

Politics

German politics are unabashedly republican and democratic, with a healthy blend of experience (Old Hans) and youth (the green party).

Food

German cuisine does not enjoy a high reputation. The hamburgers (from Hamburg) are bad, the frankfurters

---

*It is not, however, a river entirely devoid of romance. When it runs through the ancient city of Köln it is indeed known poetically as the Eau de Cologne.

(from Frankfurt) are worse, but the sausages (from everywhere) are würst. As a result the Germans are very keen on drinking – either in *Bierkellers* (or *Wunderbars*) or from off-licences (Hock shops).

Culture (Ger: Kultur)

Some words of warning.

Beware of *imitations*: many famous 'Germans' are not German at all, but Austrian. See: Mozart, Mann, Hitler, Franz Beckenbauer, Karl Marx.

Beware of *pronunciation*: many famous Germans pronounce their names infamously.

Gerter (pron. Goethe)
Wagner (pron. Vargner)
Voethe (pron. Werther)
Schiller (pron. Schiller)
Schlegel (pron. Hegel)

Wagner is perhaps the most characteristically German of German artists. His famous operas are staged during an annual Wagner Festival at Beirut (a fact that has sometimes prompted charges of anti-Semitism).

Wagner's greatest work is *The Ringcycle*, a very long opera about an early lady's bicycle ridden by the buxom and emancipated Valkyrie (pron. Walkyrie), much to the horror of the more feminine Rhine Maidens (or Siegfried Follies). Other memorable Vagnerian works (pron. vorks) include *Tristan and Iolanthe*, *Persiflage*, and *The Meisterbakers of Battenburg*.

THE RIDE OF THE VALKYRIE

THE GERMAN REICHS

The Germans have made several memorable (if deplorable) attempts to unify Europe.

Reich One (A Dark Thing)

The Old Ottonians, a group of aristocratic old Germans (all called Otto) tried to become Holy (or, at least, partly) Roman Emperor. Sadly the Dark Ages were in progress at the time so that it was impossible for them to see what they were doing. It was also too dark for them to become wholly memorable (or, indeed, Truly Roman Umpire).

Reich Two (A Bad Thing)

Otto von Bismarck (the Ironclad Chancellor) prussiarised the Kaiser into unifying Germany (which nobody had bothered to do before) and then taking over Europe. Von Bookmark even threatened to throw himself (or the Kaiser) out of the window if the Kaiser (or Von Biscuit) didn't hurry up about it. This sort of precipitous behaviour led inevitably (if indirectly) to the wholly indefensible First World War (or War To End All Wars – except, of course, the Second World War or Last War).

Reich Three (A Worse Thing)

The infamous Adolf Hitler ('The Füry') founded the despicable Nazti Party, burnt down the Reichskänzlerei, blamed it on the Communists, and thus became Chancellor of Germany. Together with his ruthless supporters (the Goebbels Diehards, the Sturm-und-Drang Troopers, the Nasty Youth Movement, etc.) he set about extending his living-room into his neighbours' back garden, with no regard for international law, common decency or, indeed, his neighbours.

This inevitably provoked the outbreak of the Second Wild War, in which Hitler was well beaten by the Allies, driven into a bunker and forced to commit suicide.

The international rules of politics, imperialism, baseball, etc. only allow you Three Reichs. If, after that, you have still failed to unify Europe you have to retire from the game. Bad luck.

HITLER – DRIVEN INTO A BUNKER

AUSTRIA

C AVEAT: Austria should not, if possible, be confused with Germany. This is difficult as the Austrians speak German and, indeed, often go on to become famous Germans in their own right (see above).

Physical Characteristics

Austria is famous for its beautiful Alpine scenery. Some of the mountains are apt to get out of hand (see the Wild Spitze and Gross Glocker), but for the most part the hills are well disposed, picturesque, alive with the sound of music, etc.

Indeed most things in Austria are alive with the sound of music. The memorable Blue Danube flows through Vienna to a strict waltztime.

Politics

Austria (Aus. *Östrich*) has an unfortunate tendency to bury its head in the sand at times of political crisis. This trait was especially noticeable – and unfortunate – during the Third Streich (see above), when Ostreich allowed itself to be annexed by Hitler during the so-called Antrobus.

AUSTRIAN POLITICS

Even their recent President, Kurt Waltztime, buried his head in the sand, started 'only obeying führers', and joined the Waffle SS. As a result Mr Warcrime is memorable – but little else.

Economy

It is highly probable that Austria has a highly profitable economy.

Culture

Austria has produced a great deal of memorable culture over the centuries.

(*a*) Music (the sound of): especially Mozart at Salzburg and Strauss at Waltzburg.
(*b*) Patisserie: strudel, sachertorte, chocolate melkshakes, etc.
(*c*) Psychology: Vienna was the home of the great psychologist Dr Sigismund Fraud, a complex man, whose seminal work 'Who's Afreud of the Dark?' suggested that all our behaviour is determined by what happens to us when we are very, very jung.

The Tyrol

This is the most memorable (and the most mountainous) part of Austria. The hills here ring not only with the happy shouts of the Von Trapp family, but also with the sound of goats, cowbells, yodelling, strudelling, and cries of 'Heidi Hi! Hoedi Ho!'

The Tyroleans are fond of music, climbing, and smoking pipes (which appear to be real but are, in fact, meerschaum). They are hard working and clean living, although there is a certain amount of idleweiss in the high pasture.

Tyrolean men are easy to distinguish because they wear lederhosen, ledershosen, lederblousen, ledersocksen and little felt hatz with feathers in them.

The Austro-Hungarian Empire
(See also Hungary)

Austria, together with Hungary, was (during the last century) part of the aptly named Austro-Agrarian Empire. This was the last remnant of the Wooly Roman Empire and was thus rather moth-eaten by this time. The Empire's symbol was a memorable Two-headed Beagle.

The Austro-Bulgarian Empire, which stretched over much of Europe, was kept together by a combination of diplomacy (the famous Hapsburg Jaw) and personal combat (the so-called Duel Monarchy).

It fell apart, however, when the Archduke Franz Ferdinand inadvertently caused the First World War by being assassinated at the hands of a black Serbian revolutionary as he drove through Saratoga in an open carriage.

EDELWEISS

TEUTONIC TEST PAPER

PART I

1. Estimate the musical, monetary *and* nutritional value of *either* 'Deutschmark, Deutschmark, über Alles' *or* 'Einer Kleine Nachwürst'.
2. Expound effusively upon the impact of the Green lobby on the smell of the River Oder.
3. Arrange in order of merit: Porz, Badheim, Wurtzburg.
4. When it comes to German rivers can you tell your Saar from your Elbe?
5. Why do the Germans call him *herr*?
6. Consider the role of the ümlaut in the rise of neo-fascism.
7. In the Mystery Play at Oberammergau – Whodunnit? And to whom?

PART II

8. What are the colours of the Old Ottonian tie?
9. Who is the hero of *From Prussia With Love*?
    (*a*) Von Bookshelf?
    (*b*) Von Blackmark?
    (*c*) Von Bondmark?
10. To what extent could it be argued that the Germans used hunfair tactics in either or both World Wars?
11. At the 1938 Olympics who took the Gold Medal in the High Jump, the 100 metres *and* the Master Race?
    (*a*) Adolf Hitler?

  (*b*) Jesse Owens?
  (*c*) Goering?
  (*d*) Streatly?
12. 'If the Nuremberg Trials were the qualifying heats for the
  Nuremberg Rally, why did they happen afterwards?'
  Discuss with reference to the ruthless deficiency of the
  Germans.

EASTERN EUROPE
(FORMERLY CENTRAL EUROPE
OR *MUDDLEUROPA*)

———

THE general muddle surrounding the whole of *Mittleuropa* is, alas, symptomatic of a deeper muddle that exists within each of the individual Mottle European countries.

Until recently this state of confusion (or confusion of states) was happily hidden from view by the Iron Curtain. Now, however, the curtain has been drawn back to reveal once again the rich muddle of Serbs, Croats, Stoats, Dalmatians, Pomeranians, West Highland Terriers, Montenegroids, Bessarabians, Slovenes, Slovaks, Slocoaches, Bohemians, Moravians, Moldavians, Bosnians, Armenians, Albanians, Ruritanians, etc.

This has caused much rejoicing among all the above, and a great deal of extra geography for everyone else.

To avoid confusion on the subject it is probably wisest to avoid *Mottleuropa* altogether. For the dedicated student, however, there follows a country-by-country guide to these old chips off the Eastern Bloc.

POLAND

Geography

Poland's geography is always changing. Other countries find it very difficult to keep abreast of these alterations and thus are often inadvertently claiming large chunks of Poland as their own.

The People

The inhabitants of this ever fluctuating country are, by contrast, very distinctive: solid, indomitable, and staunchly RC.

Politics

The old grey (or red) Communist regime has now been replaced by the very solid (if rather lecherous) Lech Warsawa and his Solidarity (Pol. *Solidarnösc*) Party.

With the return of democracy there was, of course, dancing (Pol. *Danzig*) in the streets of Gdansk (Eng. Danzig) and general scenes of wild hilarity (Pol. *hilardarnösc*).

There is, however, still lots (Pol. *Lodz*) to be done.

Economy

The Polish economy is based, rather unfashionably, on shipbuilding and cabbage growing.

VERY SOLID

Money is raised for the state by the unpopular Pole Tax.

Exports: shiploads of cabbages, a certain amount of boot polish and a few pole cats (allowing for quarantine restrictions).

Culture

The Poles are a cultured nation. They have certainly never lacked polish. Like many Central (i.e. Eastern) Europeans they have a strong tendency to be musical.

It was the Poles who invented the Polonaise, the Polka, the Itsy-bitsy Teeny-weeny Yellow Polkadot Bikini, the Mazurka and, indeed, most types of music that involve a good deal of chopin' and changin'.

CZECHOSLOVAKIA

This famous country has now (since the collapse of Communism) been renamed the Republic of Czech-and/or Slovakia. It was once, however, called 'The Coast of Bohemia' (Eng. Fitzrovia). At other times it was known variously, and in part, as Moravia, Monrovia, Moldavia and/or Pavese.

This uncertainty of nomenclature, coupled with a complete lack of notable physical features, has prevented Czech-if-not-Slovakia from becoming geographically memorable. Bad luck.

Politics

Over the years the Czech-cum-Slovaks have, however, done better than most Muddled Europeans at achieving political distinction.

- The Defenestration of Prague: several Imperial Councillors were thrown out of the Palace window into a passing garbage truck, thus causing the Thirty Years War.
- The Vexation of the Sudetenland: Hitler decided to annexe the Sudan (a Czech-not-only/but-also-Slovakian possession), thus causing the Second World War.
- The Prague Spring: the spring-cleaning reforms of President Dubczech provoked the arrival of several Russian tanks in Prague, thus (very nearly) causing the Third World War.

The election, as President, of Vaclav Halva, the noted Czech-if-not-now-when-Slovakian playwright (author of *Good Soldier Schweik*, *The Unflappable Rightness of Being President*, etc.) has proved very memorable thus far, and does not look as though it will cause a war of any sort.

Economics

There is probably a certain amount of heavy industry, well supported by heavy lunches (dumplings, lendl soup, beer, more dumplings, please, etc.).

Exports: czich peas, czocholates and Robert Maxwell.

Health Resorts

Czech-née-Slovakia is also famous for its spa towns: Karlsbad, Marienbad, Ottosnotfeelingtoowell, Vaclavsabitoff, etc.

Culture

For a small nation Czech-ivestartedsoillfinish-Slovakia has produced a great deal of culture.

Many of the most famous literary works (Cz. *Czechbooks*) display, however, strong traces of foreign influence. Alberto of Moravia and Milan Kundera belong, perhaps, to the Italian tradition. While Josef K. Kafka (who produced a rather inadequate guide book to Prague Castle before, one morning, turning into a beetle) wrote in German.

There is, however, a distinct smetering of distinctive musical culture, produced by Janaczech(-either/or-Slovak), Martinů and the famous Geordie composer, Dvořak (pron. Wor Jack).

HUNGARY

Hungary enjoys a position as 'the crossroads of Central Europe' (or 'the lost roads of Eastern Europe' or, even, 'the crossed lines of Muddleuropa').

Its capital, Budapest (not to be confused with Bucharest) stands, like most Central European capitals, on the banks of the Blue Danube. Indeed the city (which is really *two* cities) is divided by the great river, Bucha lying on this side and the rest lying on the other (or *vice versa*).

Politics

Since the great days of the Bistro-Hungarian Empire (see above under Austria), Hungary has singularly failed to come to the notice of the general public. Bad management.

Inhabitants

The Hungarians, however, have retained a high degree of memorability by being Magyars (*Eng.* Gay Hussars) and thus fond of drinking Bull's Blood and riding recklessly about on wild horses.

Cuisine

It is perhaps not surprising that a country called Hungry should have a famous national cuisine: goulash, blackcherry soup, goose liver paté, further lashings of goo, etc.

Culture

Many people go into rhapsodies about Hungarian music, and can reel off a whole liszt of native composers – such as Bartik, Bartok, Kodily, Kodály and, of course, the comic-genius Lehahar (composer of *The Blackcherry Widow*).

Traditionally Hungary has also exported film directors to Hollywood (or Pinewood). G. Cukor, T. C. Fox and all the various Kordas were, at one time or another, Hungarian.

ROMANIA

A sad country. While the rest of Eastern/Central/Mittle Europe has been getting jollier, Romania has romained rather glum. Bad luck.

A Wave of Tyrants

Rheumania has, of course, a long tradition of Bad (but memorable) Rulers:

- Vlad the Impala: a deranged and blood-thirsty Duke who waged war against the Turks, and tortured his prisoners by pretending to be a small member of the antelope family.
- Count Dracula: a deranged and blood-thirsty Count who lived in an inaccessible castle (the Hammer House of Horror) and waged war against milk-white virgins.

THE IMPALA

• President Ceaucescu: a deranged and blood-thirsty Tyrant of whom the less said the better.

ALBANIA

A backward country. Although sometimes confused with Armenia, Albania (Alb. *Ainabla*) is in fact memorable as the most backwood (and the most Communist) country in Europe. It is, as a result, bereft of many modern amenities, consumer durables, geographical phenomena, etc.

BULGARIA

Over the centuries Bulgaria has made very little effort to become either very European or very memorable. It is perhaps fortunate to be included in this book at all.

Probable History and Politics

For many years Belgravia was almost certainly part of the so-called Ottoman empire. Even now its capital is called Sofa.

After the decline of the Ottoman Empire (see also the rise of the E-Zee Reclining Lounger) Bulgaria was in all probability severely Balkanised and then swept discreetly behind the Iron Curtain.

STRONG TRACES OF OTTOMAN INFLUENCE

Culture

Yogurt and Folk Singing.

Economy

Yogurt remains a growth industry, while Folk Singers
(and Operatic Basses) are still exported. Always sensitive
to accusations of bulgarity the Bulgars have also developed a luxury trade in Attar of Roses and Balkan
Sobranie tobacco.

YUGOSLAVIA

Even by the mottled standards of *Mittleuropa* Yugoslavia
is in a terrible muddle.

Demography

The country is divided (Yug. *Splijt*) between innumerable Yugos, Slavs, Serbs, Croats, Slaves (aka Monte
Negroes), Pomeranians, etc. This has led to a lot of racial
tension, misunderstanding, sour grapes (Serbo-Croat:
Zagrebs), confusion over traffic signs, etc.

Politics

Until recently these divisions were obscured by the firm
rule of Marshal Tito. After the last war Tito and his par-
tisans (known affectionately as the 101 Dalmatians) put
the country under Marshal (Tito) Law and established a
titolitarian Communist regime.

Now, with the relaxing of Communist rule, confusion,
muddle and football hooliganism are breaking out all
over, especially in Kosovo Province.

Economy

Despite a great deal of cheap slav-labour, prices continue
to rise at an alarming rate – not least in Kosovo Province.

Culture

Some horticulture, including Kos lettuces – particularly
from Kosovo Province.

MUDDLEUROPA TEST PAPER

1. What was the Balkan Question? And what was the answer?
2. Would you holiday by the Black Sea only in the last resort?
3. Which legendary Romanian Princess was the narrator of
   The Bessarabian Nights?

4. Assess athletically the relative strengths of Hitler and Stalin as Pole Vaulters.
5. What might you expect to find in a Warsaw Pack?
6. Does the River Po run through Poland? And, if not, why not?
7. Was Josef Conrad's real name:
   (a) Josef Stalin?
   (b) Jasper Conran?
   (c) Cardinal Glemp?
   (d) Lord Jim?
8. On a scale of 1 to 10 how 'Good' was Good King Wenceslas?
9. Estimate the nationalistic and operatic impact on Czechoslovakia (and/or Yugoslavia) of:
   (a) The Stunning Little Vixen;
   (b) La Bohème;
   (c) The Bouncing Czech;
   (d) La Clemenza di Tito.
10. In the ever changing world of Central Europe just how much does Karlovy Vary?
11. Should Count Dracula be characterised as:
   (a) A blood-thirsty tyrant?
   (b) A pain in the neck?
   (c) An enlightened ruler and a much misunderstood man?
   Be as bloody-minded as you like.
12. Expatiate upon the Romance of the Romanian language.
13. Calculate the Political Credibility of:
   (a) Enver Hoaxer;
   (b) Dudcheque;
   (c) King Zog of Albania.
   Calculators may be used.
14. What (if any) was the seasonal relevance of the Radetsky March to the Prague Spring?

Modern Greece

MODERN Greece (*Hellas*) should on no account be confused with the altogether more memorable (if altogether more distant) Ancientgreece (*Alas*).

Physical Characteristics

Much of Greece is very hilly. The rest is mountainous. There are, however, only two really notable Greek mountains – Mount Olympus (inhabited by Greek gods) and Mount Athos (inhabited by Greek monks, French musketeers, etc.). The terrain is rough, dry and rather thistly (Gr. *Thessaly*)

Greece also boasts an inordinate number of highly typical Greek Islands: Samos, Lesbos, Patmos, Fulltos (where the English expatriates play cricket), Naxos, Discos, Corfu (Eng. Cor-phew), Crete, etc. These have long been popular with tourists due to their abundance of beaches, discos and tavernas, and their lack of cars (Gr. *kars*) and, indeed, roads (Gr. *rhodes*).

Politics

Since gaining their independence with the romantic assistance of Mad George Byron ('Lord, bored and gangrenous to boot') the Greeks have done little with it.

Generally speaking they have been happy (or unhappy) to dispense with General Elections and endure rule by various (unelected and unspecified) Generals of a bad and military temper.

Recently, however, they have set their sights higher and chosen a President and/or air-hostess as head of state.

Economy

The economy is based roughly on rough agriculture (olives) and crude oil (olive).

Exports: Taramasalata, humorous, fetid cheese, donor kebabs (made from unclaimed internal organs) and (the rather smarter) swish kebabs, retsina, domestos, balaclava (a sweet pudding made from woolly hats steeped in honey), and a bitta pitta bread. £10.46, not including service.

Culture

Greek culture has reached a decidedly low ebb. Any country prepared to tolerate Nana Mousaka, Demis Rousseau (brother of the more famous Jean-Jacques) and *Greece – The Musical* (starring Olivia Newton-John-Revolta) has clearly lost its marbles.

A WAVE OF GENERALS

ANCIENT GREECE

HELLAS (Ancientgreece) was the cradle of Classical (European) civilisation.

Origins

The Ancientgreeks were known as Hellenes because they all fought for Helen during the Trojan War, after she had been abducted from a Parisian nightclub and taken off to Troy (see *The Iliad*, *The Odyssey*, *Hector's House* etc.).

They were a fine warrior race, but also very wily. After their best fighter, Achilles, had to pull out of the war with heel trouble (he had been beaten in a race with a tortoise), Odysseus devised his famous wooden vaulting-horse and, concealing the army inside it, cunningly defeated the Trojans (despite all their hard work).

Political Organisation and Culture

The Ancientgreeks developed a series of city states (Gr. *Polis States*), each with its own capital (see esp. the Doric, Ionic and Corinthian capitals – in that order).

ABDUCTED FROM A PARISIAN NIGHTCLUB

Athens

Athens, however, was the most elevated city state. It gave rise to a wave of philosophers, including Aristotle (and the Peripathetics) Pluto, Socrates (or Sophocles) and various Stoics, Cynics, Mimics and Chronics.

In other areas, too, Athens led Ancientgreece (and, hence, Europe, the World, etc.).

Greek Drama was dominated by the twin figures of Sophocles (or Socrates), a master of dialogue, and Aristophanes, an irrepressible satyrist.

In Mathematics (another Greek invention), Euclid – as a rule – was always very quick to come to the point (i.e. via a straight line) while Pythagoras made the yet more memorable discovery that a square on a hippopotamus is equal to the sides of a right-tangled triangle.

Sparta

In contrast to Athens, Sparta was very spartan. Young schoolboys would allow foxes to gnaw at their vitals without thinking to mention it. This, of course, made the Spartans very brave, if rather uncomfortable.

In one celebrated incident a mere 300 Spartans took on the whole Persian Army at Totopoly, and were only narrowly beaten.

A WAVE OF PHILOSOPHERS

The Decline of Ancientgreece

Later on Sparta and Athens exhausted themselves by
waging the so-called Penelopenesian War against each
other, after Odysseus's wife Penelope had been abducted
from her weaving-frame by several over-insistent suitors.

This left the way clear for Philip of Macedon to
become 'Alexander the Great', slice through the Geor-
gian Knot (or not?), conquer India, visit the old cineaste
Diomedes (who lived in a bottle), and then die at the
romantically young age of thirtysomething. With his
death the way was clear for Ancient Rome to become the
cradle of Western Civilisation, Classical Studies, etc. (see
Italy).

GREEK TEST PAPER

PART I

1. 'The Greek Orthodontic Church lacks teeth.' Discuss this
   biting verdict on organised religion. Be incisive.
2. As a general rule, what are your feelings about Military
   Juntas?
3. Where do cretins come from?
   (*a*) Crete?
   (*b*) Behind the counter at your local Post Office?
4. How true to life is the picture of modern Athens presented
   in Coppola's *Acropolis Now*?

LIVED IN A BOTTLE

PART II

5. Discuss frankly (but poetically) the Ancientgreeks' attitude to Homersexuality.

6. Which was the least indecent of the Olympic games played by the gods on Mount Olympus?
   (a) Tossing the thunderbolt?
   (b) Follow my Leda?
   (c) 'Are You There Aphrodite?'?

7. Consider the cultural durability of either *The Iliad and The Odyssey* or *The Antigone and the Ecstasy*.

8. Which was Helen of Troy's favourite song?
   (a) 'I Love Paris in the Springtime'? *or*
   (b) 'Stand by your Menelaeus'?

9. Write all you can recall about any *three* of the following: Jason and the Huguenots; Archimedes's Screw; On first looking into Chapman's Homer; The Parthenon (or Pantheon); The Hydrant.

10. Is it fair to dismiss Paris as Helen's Troy-boy? Judge for yourself.

11. Philosophise (but not peripatetically) upon the assertion that 'The highest achievements of Classical Civilisation are to be found in the Attic.'

12. It's all Greek to me. How is it for you?

TURKEY

TURKEY is a delightful nation. But there is some doubt as to whether it is really in Europe at all (or in part). It is, nevertheless, included here on the grounds that even if it isn't quite in Europe at the moment, it might very well be at some later (or indeed earlier) date.

Physical Characteristics

In an effort to ingratiate itself with other Europeans, Turkey has very sportingly kept her physical characteristics simple and well defined.

Turkey has just one memorable mountain – Mount Arafat – where Noah's Ark ran aground, and just one memorable lake – Lake Van – where the cats like to swim in the water.

In addition the country boasts the memorable Phosphorous – as swum by Lloyd George Byron ('Damp, camp and ponderous to tow') – and the no less famous Chanterelles.

The Turks have been less successful at avoiding confusion about (and in) their capital city. It is confusedly known as Byzantium, Constantinople, Istanbul, Stamboul, Stanbowles, etc., according to taste.

MEMORABLE MOUNTAIN

Politics

Probably.

Industry

Possibly.

Agriculture

Almost certainly.

Exports: Turkish Delight; some wool from their sheep but mo' hair from their goats.

Culture

The Turkish take great delight in sweetmeats, baths, and small cups of strong coffee ('As black as night, as hot as hell and as sweet as 3–0 victory over Greece in a World Cup Qualifying Match').

History

Turkey has a good deal of History, but much of it is too confused to be usefully memorable.

During the Mittle Ages, Constantinople (named after the Roman Emperor Constantine) was the capital of the Byzantine Empire (named after Byzantium, aka Istanbul).

Soon afterwards (and probably as a result of the above confusion), Constanbul fell to the ferocious Ottoman Turks and (as Instantinople) became more thoroughly and distinctively Turkish and Ottoman (i.e. full of delightful baths, Islamic divines, Islamic divans, Hagia Sofas, etc.).

The Ottonian Turks (uttering their fearful warcry, 'Attaturk!') then proceeded to invade much of Europe (esp. Bulgaria, Hungary and other highly confused Balkan states). They even went so far as to knock at the gates of Vienna, before being soundly and roundly beaten by the Viennese navy at Levanto.

In recent times Turkish History has dwindled in significance, and now passes almost entirely unremarked.

TURKISH MINI-TEST PAPER

1. 'We found ourselves in very dire straits.' Assess this trenchant (and English) verdict upon the Dardanelles.
2. Estimate to the nearest six months the average age of *either* the Young Turks *or* Asia Minor.
3. Do you really prefer Turkish Delight to Lemon Kurd? Be sweet.
4. Who's stuffing your Turkey this Christmas?

MALTA

ALTHOUGH very small, and an island, Malta enjoys a reputation as a separate European country. It is justly famous for its small chocolate-covered sweeties and its falcons.

All countries, however, have their problems, and Malta is no exception. The Malteasers have their cross to bear. Indeed they have two crosses to bear:

(*a*) The Maltese Cross: an indigenous, home-grown cross of distinctive design.

(*b*) The George Cross: a decorative English cross awarded to all Malteasers after they had been rudely besieged during the Last War.

These crosses have, perhaps unsurprisingly, attracted waves of saints to the island:

(*a*) *The Apostles of St Paul* (see *The Acts of the Epistles*). Many of St Paul's letters were sent from the Post Office at Valetta, after he had been shipwrecked nearby.

(*b*) *The Nights of St John.* St John, too, spent several riotous nights in Malta, placing extravagant orders at the local Knightclubs, before being hospitalised.

THE NIGHTS OF ST JOHN

IRELAND

IRELAND has been known as The Republic (or Erin) since it gained its independence during an uprising at a Dublin Post Office, led by the romantic devolutionary Eamon de Guevara and his band of Black-and-Tan Shirts.

Physical Characteristics

Ireland is memorably green – except, of course, for the numerous peat bogs (Ir. *Paddy Fields*), which are brown.

It is known poetically as the 'Emerald Isle', although, in fact, it has very few genuinely precious gems. Watch out for sham rocks and the much-talked-about Blarney Stone.

The countryside boasts a full set of lakes (*loughs*), rivers (*liffies*) and amusingly named mountains (the Knockmeall Downs, Mr MacGillycuddy's Breeks, etc.).

Politics

For poetical and political purposes Ireland is divided into four provinces: Leinster, Munster, Ulster and Claridge's. And further subdivided into such memorable counties as Down, Up, Cork and Bottle.

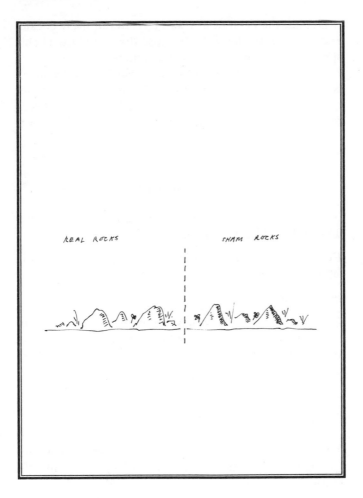

BEWARE OF IMITATIONS

Dublin, the capital, is a 'fair city' full of lively cockles and pretty muscular girls. It is also the seat of the Dial, a specially constituted circular parliament.

The Dail, presided over by the Toesock (Eng. *Oldsoak*), is the main legislative house and provides a forum for blarney, the venting of hot eire, the telling of Irish Jokes, the promoting of Green issues, the wailing of Banshees, etc.

Economics

Ireland is essentially an easy-going agricultural country. The root (or blight) of Irish prosperity is the potato.

Exports: stout beers (Guinness), stouter building-site labourers, and very fine linen napkins.

Imports: Jack Charlton.

Currency: The Irish currency, although deceptively similar to the British, should not be confused with it (esp. in your small change). Be warned: there are a lot of Irish pounds (Ir. *punts*) around (Ir. *arunt*).

Irish Sports

These esoteric old Celtic games include: shinty, haughey (pron. hockey), hurley, burley, whiskey (with an 'e'), Garlic Football and horse-racing at the Begorrah.

ROOT OF PROSPERITY

Culture

The Irish are keen preservers and promoters of their
Celtic heritage, much of which is recorded (and illus-
trated) in the famous (and illuminated) Book of Kelts at
Dublin.

Irish Poetry

The Irish have a tendency to wax poetical. Foremost
among Irish poets is W. G. Yeats (brother of the more
famous Jack Keats). William Butler Keats (pron. Yates),
having a premonition that he might be killed if he joined
the Irish Airforce, very sensibly became a poet instead.
He invented the Limerick and wrote a series of celebrated odes to Autumn, A Grecian Urn, A Night in
Galway, etc.

English Playwrights

All English playwrights since the time of Shakespeare (or
Bacon) have in fact been Irish (see esp. Sheridan, Oscar
Wilde, G. B. Shaw, Samuel à Becket).

Their plays are easily recognisable – if not easily distinguishable – on account of the distinct traces of Irish Wit.
(NB Not to be confused with Irish Jokes.)

From *The Importance of Not Speaking Erse*

Morning-room of Estragon's flat in Half Moon St, London W. Time: The Present. The room is furnished with an eye for comfort and nose for extravagance. The sound of a banjulele is heard in the adjoining room.

Lane is deranging elevenses on the table. Enter ALGERNON, GWENDOLEN, VLADIMIR, MR PUFF, DR DOOLITTLE, ETC.

PROFESSOR HIGGINS: Have you no cucumber sandwiches, man?

DOOLITTLE: Can't afford them, Guv'nor. Neither could you if you was as poor as me.

ALGERNON: Really, if the lower orders don't set us a good example what on earth are they doing in a play like this?

GWENDOLEN: Oh, Algy!

ALGERNON: Oh, Cecily! (*He sinks to his knees.*)

(*Enter* MRS MALAPERT.)

LADY MALADROIT: Arise, sir, from that semi-cucumbered posture! Come, Gwendolen, we have already missed five, if not six, trains, To miss any more might expose us to cement on the platform.

BECKETT (*Offstage, singing*): 'Happy Days are here again . . .'

LADY MACKERAL: See you later, Allegory.

ALLIGATOR: In a while, crocodile.

ELIZA DOOLITTLE (*Enunciating carefully*): Not bloody likely.

PROF. HIGGINS: Ah, a Lisson Grove burr, if I'm not much mistaken.

ALGERNON (*Ignoring these remarks*): I have invented an invaluable permanently expected friend called Godot in order that I never have to visit the country.

MR PUFF: This play is terrible. I do hope it will last.

(*Curtain.*)

CECILY: The play ends, happily. It was bad, unhappily. This is what fiction means.

VLADIMIR (*Putting on his coat*): That passed the time.

OSTROGOTH: It would have passed in any case.

LADY CRACKNELL (*Waking up with a start*): A handbag?

VLADIMIR: Yes, but not so vapidly.

THE END

IRISH TEST PAPER
(OR THE IRISH QUESTIONS)

1. How far is it to Tipperary?
    (*a*) A short way?
    (*b*) A long way?
    (*c*) Don't know?
2. Discuss with copious reference to the works of W. C. Yeats the relative merits of the Irish Airforce and the Irish Navvy.
3. Which popular song is traditionally played at Irish funerals?
    (*a*) 'Danny Boy'?

    (*b*) 'The Munster Mash'?

    (*c*) 'Wake Me Up Before You Go-Go'?

4. Consider the impact on sikh morality of J. M. Singh's *The Playboy of the Western World*.

5. If you were travelling from Meath to Louth would you be more surprised to meet:

    (*a*) a leprechaun?

    (*b*) a snake?

    (*c*) Shergar?

GREAT BRITAIN

I N 1992 Britain is going to 'Enter Europe'. The question has to be asked: Are we ready? Britain, by an accident of geography, is not very Continental. Its people are by tradition insular – a maritime breed (or Boat Race), unversed in the ways of our European neighbours (driving on the right, not eating a proper breakfast, etc.). Nevertheless, there are perhaps signs that the gap is getting narrower.

Physical Characteristics

It has to be admitted that Britain possesses less geography than many other European countries. There are no geysers, no fjords, no great mountain ranges (with the possible exception of the Crampons in Scotland) and no truly memorable waterfalls. There just isn't enough room.

Instead we have 'The English Countryside', a green and pleasant belt which surrounds the various dark satanic mills (now closed), suburban developments, new towns, international airports, and Asda superstores that take up most of the available space.

Economy

The British Economy still has many sterling qualities (just), although the currency was decimated in the 1970s to bring it into line with European custom.

Industry

Happily, very little is known about British Industry. The Conservative Government's recent policy of privation means that most of the old National Industries (British Steal, the Lost Office, Telecon, etc.) have been de-rationalised, and are now carried on privately.

Agriculture

It is also a time of change for British farming. Agriculture is becoming more and more an extension of Big Business.

British farmers now have less and less time for their traditional rural pursuits – fox hunting, hare splitting, wool gathering, and grousing about the weather. Instead they have to devote their energies to trading livestocks and shares, carrying filofaxes (esp. the Diary Farmers), fleecing the VAT man, and cultivating EC subsidies. Some farming does, of course, remain orrible, but with the emphasis on high-yield crops such as rape, oats, groats, and pop festivals.

TRADITIONAL PURSUITS – GROUSING

Politics

British politics are quite as confused as those in the rest of Europe. Indeed, many European countries have based their own Parliamentary systems on the British model.

All British political institutions are divided very neatly (and sweetly) into *two* parts. This is called the bi-caramel system of government. It is undoubtedly a good thing as it provides everyone with cheques, balances, photo-opportunities, caramels, etc. Also it prevents anything very much from being done.

The Bi-Caramel System Explained

- There are *two* Houses in Parliament – the Lords and the Commons.
- There are *two* main parties in each House – Conservative and Labour.
- There are two types of Labour MP – the moderate and the petulant.
- There are *two* types of Conservative MP – the wet (-fish) and the dry(-sherry, please).
- There are no *two* people who can remember the name of the Liberal Demagogic Social Party Party (est. membership: *two*).

Recently we have had over a decade of Conservative rule (for full details see *Our Island's Tory*). And during this time Britain has been presided over by the all-too-memorable Mrs Thatcher (Mrs T., the Iron Tea Lady, the Mother of Parliaments, etc.) who, as Prime Minister, lived (increasingly out of her depth) at Number Ten Drowning Street.

The Royal Family

Britain's Royal Family is, at present, thoroughly German in origin and thus indisputably European.

Wales (W. Cwmbyah-my-lord)

Although fervently Welsh, Wales is also proud of its links with the other Celtic (i.e. Welsh) peoples of Europe – the Bretons, Basques, Magyars, Irish, Lapps, etc.

Often representatives from these kindred peoples are invited to the great Welsh cultural festivals – or Festiniogs – there to sing and dance, eat rabbits (covered in melted cheese) and harp on about the joys of being Welsh.

Scotland (and, by extension, Northern Ireland)

Scotland (previously Caledonia stern and wild) is a very rugged and romantic country, named after the very rugged and romantic Sir Walter Scot (explorer, bird-painter, and author of the Waverley novels).*

Scotland has always enjoyed close links with Europe, especially France (see 'The Auld Appliance' or 'French Connection'). This was partly for romantic reasons

---

* A series of romantic tales about railway life, set in the Lost Property Office at Edinburgh station.

A LOCAL DELICACY

SIR WALTER SCOTT'S ILL-FATED TRIP TO THE SOUTH POLE

(Mary Queen of Scots was briefly married to a French Dolphin) and partly to annoy the English.

Culture

British culture, it must be admitted, has often shown a sorry tendency to be insular and un-European. Cricket, Carry On Films, warm beer, afternoon tea, Marmite, the *Sun*, mint sauce, Gilbert and Sullivan, Jennings and Darbishire, Morecambe and Wise, Mrs Thatcher; none of these popular British institutions has succeeded across the channel.

There are, of course, exceptions. Football, football hooliganism, Les Rolling Stones, and the comedy specials of Benny Hill can all claim to have had a profound impact on the Continent. But such instances are rare.

The tide of influence has more often run in the other direction. This is due to Classical Education, the Renaissance, the Grand Tour, Cook's Tours, Foreign Wars, Foreign Films, native indolence.

The English Poets

England is rightly proud of its poets: Shakespeare (or The Swan of Bacon), Milton, Wordsridge and Coleworth, Lard George Byron ('Mad, fat and murderous to know'), Persse Bicy Shelly, Gerard Mandy Hopkins, the Brownings (Elizabeth, Barrett and Robert), Alfred Lawn Tennyson, Sir John Bitumen. The list is impressive.

EXPORTS

Although many of the above exhibited a decidedly English sensibility (i.e. played tennys, wandered lonely as a cloud, lost things – Paradise, Love's Labour, etc.), often they drew their subject matter from Renaissance Europe (i.e. Italy) or the Classical World (i.e. Italy or, perhaps, Greece).

Many English poets even went so far as to live abroad (i.e. Italy or, at a pinch, Greece). Some even died there. Elizabeth and Barrett Browning are buried in Florence (It. *Ferrara*) together with their pet woolf, Flush. While Shelly, increasingly under the influence of drink,★ opprobrium, Byron, etc., drowned his sorrows in the nearby Gulf of La Speranza. Byron himself died in Greece, complaining that he felt, 'hot, shot and dangerously low'.

Other High Points of British Culture

The Plays of Shakespeare (aka Francis Bacon, Christopher Marlowe or what you Will): these very memorable dramas (tragical, comical, hysterical and pasteurised) contain many famous parts, including *Henry IV Part II*, *Henry VI Parts I to III*, 'Parting is such sweet sorrow', *Henry IV Part I*, etc.

The Novels of Charles Dickens: Dickens was noted for his vivid descriptions of Dickensian (and hence Victorian) London, with its smogs, fogs, fugs, Twists, turns,

★ See his 'Ode to a Nightcap': 'Hail to thee, clear spirit/Beer thou never wert.'

CAPTAIN COOKED

curiously old shops, etc. His books are all very well written (i.e. in a Copperfield hand).

The Landscapes of Constable: John Constable (or P. C. Turner) was a retired policeman who painted many scenes of a decidedly rural nature, including *The Haystack*, *A View of Salisbury Cathedral*, and *The Mill on the Floss*.

The Buildings of Sir Christopher Wren: although best remembered for designing St. Paul's Cathedral, Wren also founded the Women's Naval Service. He used to be commemorated on the farthing, but has since been promoted to the £50 note.

The Hits of The Beatles: The Beatles, with their so-called 'Mercybeat', rescued post-war Britain from being terribly dull. Instead they invented 'The Swinging Sixties', even though they themselves weren't sixty at all, but only teenagers.

Britain and Abroad

Over the years Britain has had considerable experience of dealing with Abroad. This, of course, was especially true during the Golden Age of the British Empire, when most of the map was coloured red and the midday sun never set, and the white men (together with their mad dogs) would carry enormous burdens in the appalling heat.

Most of the memorable countries in the British Empire were not, however, in Europe. New Zealand (NZ), Australia (OZ), the Cook Islands (where they cooked the

GREAT ACHIEVEMENTS

unfortunate Captain Cook), the Gilbert-and-Sullivan Islands, the Easter Islands, the Christmas Islands, the August Bank Holiday Islands: these were (and, indeed, are) all in the Antipodes.

Canada is in North America. India is, of course, in India. Rhodesia – discovered so providentially by Cecil Rhodes (*né* Cecil Zimbabwe) – is in Africa. All, alas, are far beyond the scope of this book.

Britain, however, does even now retain some decidedly European possessions:

- Gibraltar: a small and very British rock on the southern tip of Spain, garrisoned by British bobbies and Spanish monkeys.
- Tuscany: a small and very British enclave in central Italy, garrisoned with British writers and Italian hill-farmers.
- The Dordogne: a small and very British enclave in Southern France, garrisoned with the British writers who couldn't get into Tuscany (see above).

GREAT BRITAIN TEST PAPER

1. With detailed reference to the Continental origins of the Royal Family, compute the relationship between the Battenberg Cake and the Victoria Sponge.
2. Anyone for Tennyson ?
3. Using protractors and a home-ruler, estimate the relative sizes of Little Britain and Little England.

4. Is the concept of 'the Academic Marketplace' best expressed by Oxford University or Oxford Street?
5. Ruminate diligently on (*a*) cattle feed and (*b*) grass.
6. What, if anything, is the difference between:
   (*a*) Maynard Keynes;
   (*b*) Milton Friedman;
   (*c*) Milton Keynes?
   Be as economical as possible.
7. Will British Sovereignty be undermined by the Channel Tunnel – *oui ou non*?
8. Which, if either, are more vertiginous: the Wiltshire Downs or the Cumbrian Fells?
9. Who wrote *Gray's Allergy*? And what was it? Don't be rash.

AFTERTHOUGHT

RUSSIA (ANAG. USSR AI)

ALTHOUGH very largely in Asia, Russia is only a short steppe away from Poland, Czech-and/or-Slovakia, etc. and is thus in many ways very European.

Politics and History

Indeed, after the Last War, Russia tried to unify the whole of Europe by making it all part of Russia. Although this did something to sort out the confusion in Central Europe by making it all into Eastern Europe (and thus all uniformly grey and/or red), it cannot really be counted a Good Thing.

The people of Eastern (i.e. Central) Europe realised this quite early on, but it has only dawned on the Russians quite recently. So President Gorbachev – with his policy of *Gladznost* – has been busily (if not gladly) reversing this state of affairs.

Economy

Due to many years of the Communists' closed-circuit economy, Russia has become decidedly inefficient. Industry is slow, vodka is cheap, and the farmers must take collective responsibility for the bumper crop of food shortages.

Culture

The Giants of Russian literature and music have, on the other hand, long exerted a profound and beneficial influence on European Culture.

- J. R. R. Tolstoy: a Russian count who wrote *Anna Karenina*, *War and Peas*, and *The Hobbit*.
- Dostoevsky: author of *Crime And Punishment*, *The Idiot*, and *Notes from the Underground* – a guide to the Moscow metro system.
- Chekhov (R. *Tchekhov*): a tragi-comic playwright who longed to go to Moscow to visit his three sisters (Misha, Masha and Mosha), but had to stay in the country to keep an eye on his pet seagull, his Uncle Vanya, his Cherry Orchard (R. *Tcherry Ortchard*), etc. He was, not surprisingly, a master of acute observation.
- Tchaikovsky (Eng. Chaikovsky): composer of much memorable ballet music (*Swan Lake*, *Black Beauty*, *Romanov & Juliet*, etc.), which found favour even with the notoriously difficult Bolshy Ballet Company.

VERY BOLSHOI

These splendid artistic achievements are quite enough to make every awkward (R. *gorky*) young writer goggle (R. *gogol*) with wonder and admiration.

AMERICA

Some people (esp. economists, Disneyworld investors, Greenham women, telly addicts, etc.) are apt to insist that America is in fact in Europe. All too much so, indeed. Nearly all geographers, on the other hand, are agreed that America is very definitely *not* part of Europe, and is thus wholly – and happily – outside the scope of this book.

One does, after all have to draw

————————— THE LINE —————————

somewhere.